THOUGHTS ON LEAVING CAMBODIA

by

Ray Zepp

2013

Battambang, Cambodia

2013

TABLE OF CONTENTS

INTRODUCTION

This book represents the thoughts of an expatriate American who came to Cambodia in 1995 and spent thirteen years there. I spent most of my time outside Phnom Penh, which I felt from the first was not representative of Khmer culture. In my first book, *The Cambodia Less Travelled*, I wrote, "Phnom Penh – only ten minutes from Cambodia." I explored the far reaches of the country, and have visited all 200+ *districts* (srok) of Cambodia.

It has been a roller coaster ride, from the highs of successful projects helping poor people, to the lows of seeing those poor people thrown out of their homes by the landgrabbers. In particular, I have worked at all levels of the educational system for 13 years, and it breaks my heart to see the lack of learning in the system.

I also worked with many NGOs, some of which have done some outstanding work. I cite as exceptional examples around Battambang: HelpAge International, Children's Future International, and Tean Thor Association. On the other hand, I have observed both self-serving, out-of-touch international NGOs, as well as money-stealing, corrupt local NGOs. Something must be done to clean up this mess, but I fear there are too many vested interests to dent the gravy train of these organizations.

In my varied experiences since 1995, I can see clear trends in the directions Cambodia is going. As a result, it is pretty clear to me where Cambodia is headed. Consolidation of power in one political party, ownership of property by crony capitalists, Chinese hegemony, increasing gap between rich and poor: these are all observable trends that will probably become exacerbated in the next decades. I see no forces in play that might blunt these trends; in fact, there are some vicious circles that will accelerate them.

This is not an academic work. Readers will criticize its opinions and speculative conclusions. I respond by stating that my 13 years have given me the right to express my opinions about what is going on.

THOUGHTS ON LEAVING CAMBODIA

I lived for 9 years in Battambang

I came to Cambodia in January, 1995 – over 18 years ago. I left for a couple of years in 1999-2001, because after the "coup d'etat" of 1997, there were no jobs for awhile. I returned for a few more years in 2002-2005, then left for another 4 years after becoming disillusioned with progress in Cambodia. In 2009, a Cambodian friend convinced me to give it another try, so I returned for another 4 years until the present. My hopes for Cambodia have again been let down, to the point where I feel that my presence here is not producing the desired results. Indeed, it may even be that by remaining here, I, along with thousands of other expatriates, may be doing more harm than good.

I therefore want to chronicle my intellectual journey through 13 years in Cambodia, in order to document how my thinking has evolved. I am pretty negative, I admit, but I will try to point out the successes and the silver linings behind the dark clouds that appear to me to be forming over Cambodia's future.

The Legacy of the Khmer Rouge

Cambodians do not usually use the term 'Khmer Rouge'. Rather, they prefer the name of Pol Pot, as in "that happened in the Pol Pot regime," or "Pol Pot killed my father." I believe that such language is significant and indicative of the current mindset. After all, the Khmer Rouge *were* the Cambodian people, including the current leaders as well as the family next door. Cambodians had to survive the horrors of the years 1975-79, and in so doing many had to cooperate or collaborate with the Khmer Rouge in order to save their lives. Ordinary people were forced to perform unspeakable acts, such as reporting their parents to be killed in order to obtain a few bowls of rice.

The Khmer Rouge were not a conquering force from outside; they were Cambodians killing and torturing other Cambodians. There was no ethnic cleansing or sectarian hatred; people killed and tortured people just like themselves. It is hard for anyone who has met the charming, peaceful, smiling Khmer people to understand the violence and hatred of the Khmer Rouge era. But hatred there was, hiding under the surface.

During the 1960s, then Prince Sihanouk presided over what today's media paint as a golden age of Cambodia. After independence in 1954, Sihanouk embarked on a campaign of construction: schools, hospitals, roads, etc. This took place primarily in the cities, while life in the countryside remained largely as it had for the previous 2000 years. In fact, rural Cambodians began to feel that Cambodia's urban progress was being built on their backs. They resented the fact that their agricultural products – largely rice – were being taken from them, without proper recompense, to support the city folk. The Khmer Rouge rebellion in the countryside was fed by these feelings that rural farmers were getting a raw deal from corrupt, useless urbanites.

After the Lon Nol coup that removed Sihanouk, the situation was exacerbated because the Vietnam war, along with the local Khmer Rouge insurgency, forced the city dwellers to rely more and more on the agricultural products of the countryside. One might also argue that Sihanouk had held the traditional aura of the 'god-king', and as such he could command the love and respect of the peasants, even as he was exploiting them. Lon Nol did not possess this divine aura, and in fact was seen as a madman.

Thus, there was a growing hatred of the city folk by the country folk, which was used advantageously by Pol Pot. When the Khmer Rouge took over, they divided the population into the 'old people' (peasants) and the 'new people' (urbanites). The lives of the 'old people' didn't change much from earlier, while it was the 'new people' who suffered most at the hands of the Khmer Rouge.

Old rural dam built by Khmer Rouge

I dwell on this dichotomy because it appears to be happening again. The cities are improving rapidly, with five-star hotels, highways, international restaurants, night life, etc., while the rural areas are left largely untouched. No, that's not entirely accurate. The lives of many peasants are going downhill, especially as the result of 'land grabs'. I will discuss this situation a bit later.

The point is that the hatreds that allowed Pol Pot and his followers to move the peasants to overthrow the corrupt city folks are forming again. One might argue that, once again, just as revolt finally came after the political demise of the god-king Sihanouk in 1970, so revolt might again come after the death of Sihanouk in 2012.

Hundreds of articles and books have been written on the lasting effects of the Khmer Rouge. The theory of most of these is roughly that community solidarity was destroyed. Under the Khmer Rouge organization 'Angkar', people were encouraged to report their neighbors and even close family members for minor infractions, for which the miscreants would be killed and the reporter given a small reward. It was a dog-eat-dog situation, where no one could be trusted.

This lack of trust carried over after the Khmer Rouge were defeated, and many authors argue that it remains to the present day. They claim that community members do not trust one another, so that little community or group action can be taken.

I have done a lot of work with the NGO HelpAge International, and I have spent time in villages with older people. HelpAge is helping to set up Old People's Associations (OPAs) in villages in order to get villagers to help their older people. I have witnessed many old people who have been left alone, sick, dying, and friendless, possibly as a result of the Khmer Rouge dog-eat-dog villages described above. On the other hand, the OPAs are making a lot of progress in establishing community spirit. Thus, even if the Khmer Rouge years have led to mistrust, the OPAs show that such mistrust can be dispelled.

When I first came to Cambodia, 16 years after the end of the Khmer Rouge regime, the population was a psychological basket case. Virtually the entire population suffered from Post-Trauma-Stress-Disorder, or PTSD. They woke up with nightmares, went berserk in seemingly benign situations, and committed random acts of violence. There were no psychologists to care for them. They relied heavily on valium and other depressants.

Today, a person who was 10 years old in 1975 would be 48 today. The great majority of the population never experienced the KR era. However, recent research has claimed that PTSD can be passed from parents to children, and that even the present generation of young Khmers still display symptoms of PTSD. I don't actually subscribe to this theory, although I grant that some practices, such as mistrust for one's neighbor, are taught to children by parents troubled with PTSD. The one symptom that I have observed is the seemingly random act of violence. A young person who is on the surface calm and collected, will (perhaps under the influence of alcohol) toss a grenade into a restaurant or rape a 10-year old girl.

I ascribe such acts not to any latent PTSD, but to the traditional Khmer frowning on the display of emotions. The charming, smiling Cambodian who has been taught to hide his or her emotions will one day crack and burst into violence. This Cambodian personality has not changed over the centuries.

To me, the more important legacy of the Khmer Rouge era is the guilt of its victims, who were forced to perform unspeakable acts of which they could never conceive themselves capable. I could never conceive of turning in my mother to be tortured and murdered. Imagine my guilt and trauma if I actually committed such an atrocity.

It may also be that parents who feel this incredible guilt from the 1970s may turn to alcohol and valium, and may take out their stress in spousal abuse or child molestation. Domestic violence is hidden but rampant across Cambodia. Hardly a family is left untouched.

World outrage is ignited by a single rape of a young girl in India, but in Cambodia hardly a day passes without a newspaper report of a rape of a girl as young as 3 or 4. No one bats an eyelash, and rape is taken as a daily matter of course.

I also note that valium and other depressants are not the drugs of choice these days. The younger generation have taken to stimulants, especially amphetamine pills called 'yaba', and of course caffeinated energy drinks are very popular. Alcohol is being used increasingly, but I don't ascribe alcohol use to second-generation PTSD.

The other scapegoat for all Cambodia's problems is, of course, Vietnam. The Vietnamese treat Cambodians with the utmost contempt, viewing them as gullible and stupid, easy to cheat. Cambodians resent being treated as morons, and so they have hated the Vietnamese for centuries. Little wonder that they blame the Vietnamese occupation of 1979-1993 as the recent cause of many of their problems.

An interest fact about the Vietnamese occupation is that only then did the vast refugee camps spring up along the Thai border. Site II and the other camps were virtually non-existent during the Khmer Rouge era. Cambodians were not (as depicted in The Killing Fields) escaping the Khmer Rouge; they were fleeing the Vietnamese.

So in summary, despite the claims of some research, I don't really see a great lasting effect of the Khmer Rouge era. Cambodian society, from what I read, has remained pretty much constant and hasn't changed much from what it was in 1960.

The Post-UNTAC Hope

When I came to Cambodia in 1995, hopes were running high. The world was praising the success of the UNTAC elections in 1993, which were described as largely 'free and fair.' Cambodia had a freely elected democracy. The people had finally thrown off the successive yokes of the Khmer Rouge and the Vietnamese. They were now free and looking forward to getting their lives back into order after decades of chaos. We have all seen the photographs of long lines of eager voters lined up to vote in the UNTAC elections.

Nevertheless, the post-election period showed some serious defects:

1. The Khmer Rouge remained a force around Cambodia, and actually controlled large tracts of the country. They had pulled out of the election and continued to carry out acts of terrorism from their bases in Anlong Veng and Pailin.
2. The losing party, the Cambodian People's Party or CPP, threatened to split Cambodia in two, so the UN capitulated and allowed the government to have two prime ministers and two ministers for each department.
3. The winning royalist party, FUNCINPEC, didn't display great leadership. Prince Ranarridh, the 'first' Prime Minister, was seen as cultured but ineffective.

Still, in the spirit of optimism, people felt that these obstacles could be overcome. After all, hadn't the Khmer Rouge and Vietnamese been overcome? Now that foreign aid and international expertise were flowing into Cambodia, surely the future was bright.

I came to Cambodia on a USAID-sponsored project to help revive the university system. I taught marketing research, and placed my students in projects with new businesses in Phnom Penh. There was tremendous enthusiasm among students and employers. As these students were the first to graduate in several decades, they represented the future of Cambodian business. To this day, most of the top marketing managers around Cambodia are my former students from 1995-97.

I was able to travel around Cambodia to places that foreigners had not visited in decades. It was an exciting time to pioneer tourism in unknown areas. My writing, notably *The Cambodia Less Traveled*, was in stark contrast to the mainstream writing of the time by war correspondents. It was to their advantage to portray Cambodia as a dangerous, land-mine infested hell-hole, since this portrayal had been their bread-and-butter. I wanted to show a different side of Cambodia – the pleasant people, the scenery and tourist attractions, the Buddhist temples, etc.

The 'coup d'etat' of 1997 was a rude awakening to many people, both foreigners and Khmer. It showed everyone that the leaders were interested in their own power, not the development of Cambodia. Most Western media blame Hun Sen for grabbing power, but both sides were at fault. In fact, it is now clear that Ranarridh, not Hun Sen, started the war, even though it can be argued that he was forced to do so. Each side had been negotiating with the dreaded Khmer Rouge to overthrow the other side. Cambodians could hardly believe that its elected rulers were trying to bring the KR back into power.

If you read Cambodian history over the past millennium, you will observe the common pattern of two internal parties vying for power by inviting in the bad guys from neighboring countries. One faction would invite in the Thais to help them overthrow their rivals, and when they won, the other faction would invite in the Vietnamese to help them to regain power. Thus, the events of 1997 can be seen as typical of Cambodian politics.

Foreign NGOs and other agencies pulled out of Cambodia in 1997 and stayed away for a few years. There was a feeling of gloom. The ruling CPP was composed of former Khmer Rouge leaders who had opportunistically switched sides and had ruled as Vietnamese puppets. Hun Sen, Chea Sim, and other current ministers are still the old guard of communists from the Heng Samrin regime. The Khmer Rouge leaders – Pol Pot, Khieu Samphan, Ieng Sary, and Nuon Chea – were still at large. Some of them were allowed by the CPP government to control Pailin with its gemstones and timber, probably as reward for their support in the 1997 events. Pol Pot died, of course, but the others have still not been brought to justice by the KR Tribunal, which has now become pretty much a joke, as the CPP continues to protect its former allies from prosecution.

The period after 1997 was peaceful under CPP control. There was a bushfire war on the borders with the remnants of FUNCINPEC, but eventually Ranarridh agreed to join a coalition government. The government needed to make him appear to be part of the government, so they basically invented the meaningless 'Senate' just to give him something to be the head of.

By 2000, everyone was fairly happy: the CPP was in charge, the KR had been largely defeated, and a semblance of democracy was in place. NGOs returned and started pouring money again. Multinational companies began to feel that Cambodia was a safe place to do business.

Still, there were clouds on the horizon. One came in the form of a new face on the political scene: Sam Rainsy. He made all the right noises to the Americans and Europeans. He was the face of democracy as he railed against the anti-democratic practices of the government. He was the darling of the West. What the West ignored was Rainsy's strongly racist anti-Vietnamese stance, which he used to whip up public sentiment. After all, wasn't Hun Sen the puppet of the Vietnamese?

Hun Sen could not tolerate this opposition. In an action almost unanimously ascribed to Hun Sen, grenades were thrown at an opposition rally, killing several Sam Rainsy supporters. The perpetrators were allowed to escape by nearby police, and they fled inside a CPP-controlled compound. Hun Sen blamed Rainsy by stating, incredbly, that Rainsy should be arrested for standing in a place where the grenades landed. Since an American was among the injured, the FBI was brought in to investigate, bringing international attention to the murders, and hence, disrepute on Hun Sen. No one has ever been arrested for the murders, as the government has been able to stifle all investigation.

A second storm cloud was the growing corruption at all levels. It was becoming clear that high and low government officials were interested only in enriching themselves at the expense of the rest of the country. Police stopped motorists to extract bribes. People bought their jobs regardless of their lack of qualifications. Children were not able to attend 'free' public school because their teachers demanded bribes. Judges decided court cases on the basis of which side paid the higher bribe. Corruption threatened to engulf the entire nation, as everything was for sale.

The population saw their hopes of a free, democratic society going up in smoke. There was widespread disenchantment with the system. However, no one wanted to return to the war and chaos of the Khmer Rouge period, so they tolerated more and more abuse. As long as there was no war, they paid their bribes and joined into the corruption.

My own personal experience was pushing me into pessimism. I spent most of my time in the fields of education and charity development work. In both cases, I was sorely disappointed. I will go into greater detail on these topics later, but let me comment briefly here.

Corruption had invaded education to such an extent that I could see no learning taking place. Students cheated and purchased grades and diplomas, without learning anything. A high school diploma or a university degree meant nothing. How could I, a lifelong teacher, participate in a system where my students were not expected to do any homework or learn anything?

I worked a lot with both small, local charities and big, international NGOs. Both left me disappointed, for slightly different reasons.

I spent a lot of time helping local NGOs to write project funding proposals and evaluation reports. I came to see that most of these proposals were just attempts to get money, despite the fact that these local NGOs called themselves 'non-profit organizations.' The money obtained was embezzled and the designated beneficiaries –

orphans, HIV patients, indigent elderly, poor children – had their benefits stolen from them by the NGOs.

At the same time, I saw the international charity organizations as self-serving operations bent on feathering their own nests at the expense of their beneficiaries. I will have more to say later.

As a result of my disillusionment, I left Cambodia in 2004 and spent 4 years in other countries: Uganda, Qatar, and Turkish Cyprus. In 2008, a former Cambodian student contacted me and enticed me to return to Cambodia to set up a new university. He convinced me that there was a growing class of Cambodians who wanted a real education. They realized that their future depended on their skills and ability to do the job, rather than their ability to buy their future jobs. There appeared to be a large number of middle class and upper class Khmers who would pay actually to learn the skills needed for their future.

So I returned, with a vision of a university guided by a philosophy of 'learning by doing'. Over the past 4 years I have had some good students who have been interested in learning. However, the great majority of students are so inured to the present corrupt system that they have no interest in actually studying and learning things.

My vision for education has, alas, proved too idealistic. It's going to be a long time before Cambodians begin to believe that their future is determined by what they can do, not by how much they can pay. I am getting old and cannot wait decades for Cambodia to get its act together. Meanwhile, they are falling farther and farther behind their neighboring countries and the rest of the world.

So Why Have I Stayed So Long?

As I have watched the political, economic, and educational systems deteriorate, you may ask what has kept me here so long. The quick answer is that life in Cambodia is easy.

And cheap.

I stay in a hotel in Battambang for $240 per month. I have air-conditioning, cable TV, internet connection, maid service, fridge, back-up generator, etc. If anything goes wrong, such as a   I just tell the management and they fix it. I don't have to pay for utilities, furniture, bedding, or anything. I don't worry about security as long as I keep my important documents locked up.

I eat well in Battambang. There are several expat restaurants, as well as some very good Khmer places to find a wide variety of delicious, cheap food. I ride a bicycle around town and to work, but hire a motorcycle for trips to the countryside. I have good friends, both expat and Khmer. On Friday nights I go to the wonderful Riverside Balcony Bar. (Their new sign says the Ballony Bar, but John, the Australian owner, has decided it's a good joke to keep it that way.) There are art galleries, a book club, a philosophy club, a couple of movie nights, and other activities to keep expats from getting bored.

It's no wonder, therefore, that expats get used to the easy life here and stay on despite the political shenanigans. In fact, the successful long-termers are those who can tune out the politics, keep their heads down, and hunker down into their private lifestyles. I know several male expats who have married lovely local women and spend their time and energy on their house and family, rather than getting involved in local issues.

A second thing that has kept me here is the work. I love my students and enjoy preparing and teaching classes suitable to their needs. This certainly keeps me from getting bored, and it also makes me even eager to go to class every day. It makes me feel, despite my negative attitudes towards the educational system, that I am contributing to Cambodian education and helping a few students to improve themselves.

Finally, Cambodia is so interesting! It's culture, history, language, geography, tourism, and people have fascinated me from the moment I arrived. It's a country like no other.

EDUCATION

The University I helped to set up in Battambang

Cambodia in 1995 was an exciting time for educators like me. The educational system had been destroyed over the past three decades and was virtually non-existent. Those involved in the reconstruction were thrilled to be able to start from scratch and to implement the modern educational theories and practices that would lay the foundation for Cambodia renaissance.

I was part of a project to restore the Faculty of Business (an odd title, since it was an independent entity, not a 'faculty' of any university), which had been run by the Vietnamese for the past decade. Classes were taught by Vietnamese in the Vietnamese language, and had no relationship to the 'business' courses usually taught at Western universities. Rather, it was the old Marxist-Leninist cant common to the old communist regimes.

My students were similar to the famous Chinese 'Class of '85' , where the most brilliant of all those students who had been denied an education during the Cultural Revolution suddenly appeared in classes, eager to get ahead, and confident of their future. Similarly, many of our Cambodian students were the cream of the crop. We had no doubt that many of them would become the future leaders of the country.

Our students and co-teachers were keen to learn about Western management practices. My marketing research classes were a revelation to them, as were my on-the-job methods like doing real market research projects for local companies. Not all of them, of course, were willing to adapt to the new kind of education. Some held fast to the old methods, and resorted to cheating and corruption to get through.

Primary and secondary education was in even worse shape, since many of the schools had been destroyed and there were no trained teachers. The bankrupt government could afford to pay teachers less than a dollar a day, so teachers had to work at other jobs to make ends meet. Still, many of these teachers felt a sense of commitment to rebuilding the youth of Cambodia. There was an optimistic feeling that something could be done.

Unfortunately, it quickly became clear that government officials were more interested in getting rich quickly than in improving the educational system. Teachers saw that they would not be treated as professionals any time soon and that their sacrifices would not be recognized. They became part of the same corrupt system in which, in order to survive, they would demand bribes of students and resort to other self-enriching practices. "Ghost teachers" began to appear on the rolls; a teacher whose name was on the roles would take another job and either not show up for work or else pay an unqualified teacher to take his or her classes.

It was discouraging to note that public schools had no operating budget other than teachers' salaries (which were often delayed for months or even years). That meant that every piece of chalk or paper, not to mention desks, blackboards, and building repairs, had to be paid for by the students. In poor areas (i.e. almost all areas of the country), poor children could not afford to attend school, which was advertised as 'free public education'.

The public universities, notably the Royal University of Phnom Penh (RUPP) were well known to be pretty useless, and the students knew it. As a result, a large number of private universities began to spring up. Norton was the first of these. I taught for a year at one of the new private universities, another exciting start-up with a lot of promise, since the founder and president promised that it would be a real university with international standing. Once again, my hopes were dashed. The president was just a pompous fool who liked to strut around with "I am a university president" written all over his face. In the end, it was just another money-spinner, designed to separate students from their cash and give them a worthless piece of paper. The real tragedy is that a worthless piece of paper is all the students wanted, and were willing to pay for.

Another strange educational experience was working for a couple of months for Maharishi Vedic University (MVU), way out in the boondocks of Prey Veng Province. They are the group who promote transcendental meditation, so all their students practiced TM before classes in the morning and after classes in the afternoon. It was all pretty mumbo-jumbo, but somehow they turned out good students. There were several Australian volunteer teachers, and in the small village there was nothing to do in the evening but study and learn. I spent many interesting evenings drinking coconuts with the students, who were all too eager to engage in all sorts of interesting conversations. I kept in touch with some of these students, and learned that they all succeeded in getting good jobs, I suppose because they, unlike most Cambodian university graduates, actually had learned some useful skills.

As a volunteer at MVU, I received free meals and a small stipend. I was prepared to spend another month with them, when they asked me to do a research project with a team of students. I jumped at the opportunity and we turned out a very good research report. During the write-up in the office, I happened to see the project document, and learned that the donors were giving MVU $150 per day for my services. They were secretly raking off a huge profit from my services, but since I had agreed to work on a volunteer basis, I had no cause for complaint.

I remained on good terms with MVU, but after my departure, the usual tales of corruption surfaced. The President was implicated and forced to resign. In the end, the grossly underfunded MVU was taken over by the government and began the Chea Sim (long-time president of CPP) University.

I worked for an NGO that was setting up the school system in a remote area of Cambodia, the last redoubt of the Khmer Rouge. It was a wonderful experience. My dedicated Khmer team and I visited the new schools and new teachers to put on teachers' workshops and to coach the new school principals. We saw a lot of the usual corruption – ghost teachers and ghost students, all designed to funnel money into the pockets of officials. But we felt that we were doing a very fine service in places where there had been no education at all in over 30 years. The schools were still vastly underfunded, run mostly on student 'unofficial' fees, but thousands of students were showing up for classes.

In many of our school visits, we would show up only to find the students running around the playground with no attending teacher. Sometimes the absences were legitimate, especially from illness, notably malaria, which was rampant in the area. Sometimes the entire school would have to shut down due to a malaria outbreak. But more often, the teacher was off working another job, or was attending a wedding or funeral. The District Director of Education owned the only shop selling school supplies, so the schools were forced to buy from him. Talk about a conflict of interest!

Another observation was that most of the principals and many of the teachers were disabled, usually missing at least a leg. They had been injured during the many years of warfare and could no longer do manual work. They became school principals and teachers, and they did a wonderful, committed job since there was not much else they could do. They were the backbone of the educational system there.

A few good people can go a long way, but they cannot correct the basic problem in public education: the lack of funding. As long as poor children are forced to pay unaffordable bribes to attend school, the system will not change much.

Naturally, the government cannot admit that its biggest problem— bribery -- even exists. I recall attending a conference (lavishly funded by donors) where a highly paid consultant presented his solution to the low enrolment: an advertising campaign to convince parents to send their kids to school. Thousands of pretty posters were printed and posted around the countryside, all to no avail. At the conference, I suggested that children were not enrolling because they couldn't afford it. The 'expert' could only say "That's Bullshit," hardly a common expression for a formal conference.

Despite our work with some fine people in the remote province, the other half of the job – the administration in the NGO office in Battambang -- was not so encouraging. Here we had to deal with self-serving, bureaucratic foreigners who seemed to delight in criticizing our work. Whatever we did, it would be wrong, even when we returned proud of our accomplishments. Our project director was constantly contradicting herself, telling us to do one thing, and when we did it, telling us she had told us to do the opposite. It was a schizophrenic existence, thinking we were doing a good job in the field, only to be told we were doing it all wrong.

I have written about the famous high-jump pits many times, but it is such a good story that it bears repeating. It shows how the 'experts' can go horribly wrong. In fact, the following is the entire article that I wrote for the Bayon Pearnik.

THE FAMOUS HIGH JUMP PITS OF SAMLOT

A True Story

First, there was no demand for such pits. There is no tradition of jumping at primary schools, and most children have never heard of such a thing. But some expert, undoubtedly attempting to raise educational standards, decided that a high jump would be a good idea. S/he probably approached the local authorities and asked whether they needed a high jump pit. Of course they said yes, not looking a gift horse in the mouth and thinking they might rake off some profit from the deal. So the agreement was drawn up.

Next came the detailed planning, using a logical framework format complete with objectives, inputs, expected outputs, timelines, etc. A highly paid consultant was probably brought in from France to state the correct measurements of high jump and long jump pits, and s/he very professionally consulted the official handbook for the correct measurements. Somehow, the measurements were taken for a professional Olympic pit, not for primary school children. So the lowest rung of the high jump bar was set at 1.50 meters. One can just imagine a 90-cm first grader looking up at that 1.50 m bar and being told to jump over it. Likewise, the long jump pit was so far away (10 m) that no primary student could ever jump even halfway towards the pit.

So the construction began. A hole was dug. Professional quality sand was brought in to fill the hole and to create a track for the run-up to the long jump. But no one could build up much speed trying to run through deep sand. Moreover, the designers forgot that the run-up to the high jump is negotiated from the side, not head-on. They therefore forgot to build run-up tracks to the side for the high jump.

The pit was built at the end of the dry season. When the rains began, the pit quickly filled up with water. As the sand gradually was dispersed, the pit became a mudhole. Moreover, the school grounds were the grazing grounds of many cattle, who proceeded to use the pit as a toilet. A well-placed cow pat happened to end up in just the spot where a jumper might land. Surely children in their school uniforms, especially girls in their school skirts, were not going to jump into this mixture of mud and cow manure.

The pit could not be used. Weeds grew up in and around the pit. It was forgotten. The NGO had some nice photographs of the pit when it was new to show to the donors. After the total failure of the first pit, the NGO decided to go ahead and construct another 13 pits like it in order to treat other schools in the District fairly. So there are now 14 unusable mud/manure holes at the various primary schools in Samlot District.

And the cost? How much does it cost to dig a hole and fill it with sand? Estimates of the amount paid to the constructor vary from 400 to 900 dollars. If one considers the fees paid to the highly paid expatriate consultants who planned and designed the pits, the cost of each pit must be nearly 1000 dollars. Now let's put this $1000 into perspective. A primary teacher receives a salary of 25 dollars per month, or 300 dollars per year, so the cost of the pit could pay the salaries of at least three teachers for a year. Or again, the total non-salary operating budget for an average sized school s about 500 dollars per year. Thus, the money spent on one pit could have bought enough paper, pens, and other school supplies to last the school for nearly two years.

As a further example of how this fantasy world of NGO experts develops, consider what happened next. The planners had pleasant mental images of sports instructors teaching sports to happy pupils, so they decided to run a two-week training course for the physical education instructors. Trouble is, there were no such instructors ("Don't worry, we'll find some.") They randomly selected 25 'physical education instructors' and had them do calisthenics and play volleyball in the heat of the April afternoon. Were there any complaints from the schools? Of course not. They received their per diem payoff from the NGO, and returned to their schools, where of course there still no classes in physical education of sports.

Next up… round up some teachers for dancing lessons (true!)

Well, I left Cambodia for four years. In other countries I witnessed novel ways in which governments were politicizing the educational system. The Qatar government was throwing money and foreign consultants at its educational system, which continues to have some of the lowest science and mathematics results in the entire world. In Turkish Cyprus, I saw an admissions policy that admitted students from mainland Turkey who could not be admitted to Turkish universities. In order to 'Turkfy' its half of the island, the Turkish government was allowing thousands of its worst students to attend high-cost private universities in Cyprus, quite a money-spinner for those universities, which were springing up like mushrooms.

So maybe, I thought, Cambodia was not so bad. A former Cambodian student of mine had been named Director of a new university in Battambang. He invited me to return to Cambodia to help set up this promising university. His cogent argument was that Battambang had a growing middle class who wanted a higher quality education than they were getting at the local degree mills. We would create the first real university in Cambodia. Alas, he had painted too optimistic picture to the university shareholders, and when the number of students did not reach their expectations, they threw him under the bus and reverted to the usual Cambodian model.

All this happened during a four-month period during which I was on a leave of absence in Phnom Penh, working on setting up the new World Bank Higher Education Project. This work proved revealing from an insider's viewpoint. The WB was trying to improve Cambodia's chronically defective higher education system. Their multi-pronged strategy included what you might expect: faculty scholarships for higher degrees, improvement of research capacity, scholarships for poor students, adapting curriculum to labor demand, etc. But how to do all this? The usual solution is to hold workshops and seminars for higher educators around the country.

The hidden agenda behind all these workshops, however, is the famous DSA, or Daily Subsistence Allowance. This is a *per diem* allowance for participants in all these workshops. Faculty and government receive very low salaries, so DSA represents a substantial percentage of their income. Most foreign assistance in all fields usually boils down to DSA perks for officials. It gets the big foreign donor bucks into the pockets of local officials in a legitimate way.

Another thing I learned about at the World Bank was the rivalry between the Department of Higher Education (within the Ministry) and the separate Accreditation Committee of Cambodia (ACC), situated within the Council of Ministers. This represents a bizarre situation where Ministry officials have no control over the accreditation (and hence the curriculum, methods, and quality) of the higher education they are supposed to represent. There are many gray areas where it is not clear which agency has control over which policies. The situation is caused by and exacerbated by the fact that the Council of Ministers is presided over by one of Hun Sen's closest and most powerful cronies, Excellency Sok An.

I should mention that the title 'Excellency' is an honorific towards which most Cambodians aspire. However, if you pronounce the Khmer word 'aekodóm' incorrectly, as 'aekmodóm', the meaning is 'piece of shit.' Attempt to call someone 'aekodom' at your peril.

The need for accreditation was evident by 2000, when the proliferation of universities and programs was chaotic. There was a real need to place some accountability and standardization of higher education programs. Unfortunately, the control over university programs went to the opposite extreme, and now allows almost no creativity in higher education. Universities are in a straitjacket as to what they can offer. The length of term, number of hours per course, and even the syllabi of the courses are dictated by the ACC.

Moreover, the ACC is composed mostly of politicians, not educators. I had difficulty explaining some university courses to regulators who had no idea what I was talking about. I recall trying to justify offering a course in Cultural Anthropology, and was asked, "What's anthropology?"

While I was in Phnom Penh, things went pear-shaped for my colleague in Battambang, who was forced out of office. Undaunted, he asked me and a few other educators whether we would like to set up our own private university. We were still convinced that middle and upper class families would still prefer an education that offered such unheard-of novelties as homework, standards, lack of cheating, accountability, etc. So we launched Dewey International University, named after the American education whose philosophy was 'learning by doing.' We are in our fourth year of operation and haven't gone under yet. In fact, we are thriving, for reasons described below.

We had initially intended to operate only a university without K-12 classes. We pinned a lot of hopes on a 2-year diploma program, which was advertised as "Jobs! Jobs! Jobs!" Our aim was to offer the job-oriented courses like accounting, English teaching, or NGO work, without all the general university courses like history, economics, and science.

The diplomas were a total failure. Students wanted a full degree. They preferred a Bachelor's degree in which they learned nothing to a skills diploma where they actually learned something.

We decided to open an 'International School' with classes from kindergarten through grade 12. Mornings were devoted to the normal Khmer curriculum, while afternoons were all in English for our American curriculum. The great success was the morning Khmer curriculum, probably because we brought in a well-known principal who ran a tight ship in the traditional manner. There were points of conflict, for example, when some of our liberally-trained Western teachers saw the old principal beating students and inflicting other harsh punishments. The parents are used to those methods, and approved heartily by sending more and more of their children to our school.

Meanwhile, a lot of our Bachelor's Degree students were dropping out, mostly, in my judgment, because we expected them to do homework. They were expecting the usual purchase of a meaningless piece of paper, and we (gasp!) expected them to learn something. Mind you, we have many serious students who are interested in learning. I really enjoy having them in class. But we do not get the huge numbers of students to fill our classes. Other local universities pack 50-60 students into a classroom and make lots of money, while we have to settle for at most 25. Thus, our BA programs are not big money-spinners like our K-12 programs are.

One bright spot of our programs has been our work with local NGOs. We have signed MOUs with many organizations which either place students in internships, or set up research projects in which both students and teachers can participate. We have lived up to our motto of 'learning by doing' and teach courses in Community Service Learning. Students really appreciate these projects and learn a lot about conditions in poor villages.

I had hoped that an emphasis on social responsibility would attract students into our Faculty of Social Sciences. This was not the case. Cambodian students want primarily to study Business. When questioned in greater depth, they picture themselves as sitting behind a desk in an air-conditioned office, telling subordinates what to do. This is the image of the 'manager'. When asked, "What do you want to manage?" they have no idea what to answer.

Similarly, many students want to become accountants. Indeed, in some universities more than half the students are accounting majors. I'd like to know what they are learning, because I have taught mathematics courses to some of them, and they appear to know nothing about business math. Compound interest? Present value? Forget it. Many of them cannot even calculate a percentage increase or decrease, and I have witnessed some who haven't even mastered the concept of division. And these are accountants?

It's almost unbelievable how mathematics (my major subject) is neglected in Cambodia. To my knowledge, not a single one of the ninety-odd universities has any mathematics or statistics majors, nor do any of them offer even elementary calculus. "College Algebra" (read "junior high school algebra") is offered in most Foundation Year programs, but I haven't seen any evidence that any university graduates can solve a simple linear equation.

Mathematics is probably the worst example of know-nothingness, but the same applies in other disciplines. I talk to teachers who are appalled at what their students have not learned. For instance, I know that my current literature students have just finished a course in "Comparative Religions" When I asked them what the holy book of Islam was, not a single student had any idea, and even after I mentioned the Koran, no one had ever heard of it. What on earth has been going on during the 45 contact hours of "Comparative Religions?"

One has to ask, "How can this be possible?" Why are students flocking to universities, only to spend four years learning nothing? I think that a possible answer is that hiring in Cambodia has nothing to do with a candidate's knowledge or skills. Jobs are obtained either by straight purchase or by insider contacts, such as through families or old-boy crony networks. The bachelor's degree is a written prerequisite for a job, or else an employer wants to present a façade of respectability, so he hires a family connection with a university degree just for show. Any skills required for the job can be taught on-the-job. That explains why a job-oriented diploma is of no value in the employment marketplace.

Here's an unbelievable result of a recent UNDP survey around the world. The survey asked many questions, including whether people think their country has a good educational system. Cambodians were *first* among all countries in the world in high marks for their educational system. The country with perhaps the most dysfunctional educational system in the world believes that its system is the best.

Cambodians seem to living in a make-believe world regarding their education. They are just going through the motions of attending classes and receiving degrees without learning anything, but they are quite happy with the system. It is hard to foresee any changes in a system which Cambodians view as the best in the world.

The Cambodian economy is apparently booming. Hotels and other buildings are popping up every day. They require engineers and construction experts. Where are these technicians being trained? Clearly not in Cambodian institutions of higher education like universities. Will we see buildings collapse like the recent catastrophe in Bangladesh? Let's hope not. And what about doctors? Who is staffing the medical sector? None of my colleagues would ever visit a Cambodian-trained doctor. I did -- once.

And yet Cambodia has not collapsed and is stumbling along. I am forced to think blasphemous thoughts, such as, maybe, just maybe, the entire global higher education system is worthless, and that billions of students, paying trillions of dollars, are just being conned. Maybe the only real learning is on-the-job training. How many mathematics graduates, for example, have ever had to solve a differential equation in real life? How many political science graduates have ever had to apply the theories of Hobbes, Locke, or Rousseau? Perhaps Cambodia, if it succeeds in its economic development, is proof of the uselessness of a university degree.

Maybe as a university educator, I have just been wasting my time. Maybe the Cambodians know what I have failed to realize, that it doesn't matter whether you learn anything in university. You get your job first, possibly by buying it or through your uncle, and *then* you learn how to do the job. That thought is a major reason why I am retiring from Cambodia and from higher education in general.

NGOs

Teaching English to poor children at Tean Thor Association

Every year there is a donor conference in Phnom Penh. All the major donors meet to coordinate their aid to Cambodia. Every year they begin by scolding Cambodia for its worsening human rights record and corruption. The government then promises to get its act together and respect human rights and fight corruption. Then the donors decide to increase their aid by another 100 million dollars, providing the government keeps its promises. When the donor conference is over, the government ignores its promises, corruption gets worse, and human rights are stepped on, until next year's donor conference, where the same scold/promise/increase-aid cycle begins anew. I have observed this repeated circus since 1995, and it would be a joke, if the stakes weren't so serious.

Foreign governments and NGOs are turning a blind eye to the government's atrocities. Why? Because they believe that increased aid gives them influence and leverage over the government. Their irrefutable argument? "If we didn't supply that aid, the government would be even more corrupt." The ruling party murders a dozen opposition candidates? Without a billion in aid, they would murder two dozen. Thus, government performance goes down, down, down, while foreign aid goes up, up, up to prevent government from going down further.

In the past few years, orphans have become the growth industry around Battambang. On one road just outside Battambang there are four orphanages in a row, all with names containing the word "hope". Tales are told of big Land Cruisers driving up to orphanage schools in the morning and depositing two or three 'orphans' for free education from foreign teachers.

There are basically two types of NGOs: small local organizations who apply to international donors for funding, and large international organizations with their own funding. I have worked extensively with both types.

I learned a lot about the NGO industry years ago, when I supervised a project run by a local NGO and funded by an international religious organization. We hired an on-site Englishman to help the project manage their project, write reports, and distribute benefits to poor people. On one hand, the NGO handed in their monthly receipts to me, while on the other hand, the on-site distributor handed in lists of what actually went to the poor people. It turned out that the NGO was writing false receipts for six times the amount that was actually going to poor people. In other words, for every six dollars of the project, one went where it was supposed to go and the other five into the pockets of the NGO director.

I also witnessed other tricks. The NGO had four or five projects from different donors, and they managed to charge their rent and overhead to all the donors, making a profit of four times their rent.

They also had personnel receiving full-time salaries from several donors.

The on-site Englishman reported these corrupt practices. The local NGO actually poisoned him so that he was hospitalized, and they further intimidated him so that he resigned for fear of his safety.

What was interesting was the reaction of the religious donor. They did not want to believe that they were being cheated to such an extent. Luckily, at the end of the project, the NGO was not renewed, but they got away with the money they had stolen.

A couple of observations are in order. First, the donor, which receives its donations from little old ladies going to church on Sunday, does not want to report corruption for fear of losing its donations. They turn a blind eye to the worst practices in order to project their rosy outlook. No wonder that when reports are written by NGOs, all projects are great successes and no corruption is ever discovered. The donor agency becomes an accomplice of the corrupt NGO in order to keep the donations flowing.

Another common practice is to register project land, vehicles, and other tangible assets, in the name of the individual director. This practice is abetted by government policy, which makes it virtually impossible to register property in the organization's name. At the end of the project, the director owns the assets. Similarly, microfinance projects receive initial funding from outside donors, but at the end of the project, the money returns not to the donor but to the local NGO, which is usually a one-man-show anyway, so the director makes off with the money.

Second, the NGO director in question was very good at convincing donors to fund his projects. He would take them to a village with blind and otherwise handicapped peasants working on a 'self-help project', and the donor representatives would be reduced to tears while they reached for their wallets. After the donor later learned of his corruption and discontinued funding, he simply repeated the performance for other donors, who agreed to fund his projects. No donor ever checked on his previous corruption, so he continued to attract donors, steal their money, lose their funding, and then convince new donors who didn't do their homework.

There is no cooperation among donors or NGOs. Indeed, they are rivals, competing for the same dollars. Sometimes two or more NGOs get funding from different donors to do the same type of project in the same village. Again, it is a win-win situation where everyone is satisfied. The villagers are getting double benefits, and each donor agency gets its glossy photos of helping the villagers.

Third, even if the local NGO steals 5/6 of the money, the poor people at least receive something. Without the project they would receive nothing. It is a win-win-win situation: the poor get some benefits, the NGO makes out like a bandit, the donor gets to show pretty pictures of poor people receiving benefits and the little old ladies feel happy that they are helping the poor natives. Why should anyone want to change such a situation?

This third argument is a version of the "first, do no harm" logic. The donors are helping some people, even though a lot of the money goes into other pockets, but where is the harm in that? One must be careful of this argument. Here is an example:

A local NGO run by foreigners whom I find totally trustworthy and trying to do 'the right thing' has attempted to send poor children to public schools by paying their bribes. At least the children are getting an education that way. However, the NGO directors found that the poor students were being discriminated against and treated as second-class students. School was a very negative experience for these children. In the end, the NGO directors decided to pull the children out of public school, and so they set up their own school.

That leads to another serious question: if the government refuses to provide adequate education to children, should foreigners step in and do the government's work? Worse, I have observed many instances where foreigners have done the government's job, and the government has taken full credit for the work anyway. For example, when a donor puts up a new school, it is often called a 'Hun Sen School', as though Hun Sen himself had funded it. If a donor agency builds a new road, the ruling political party claims credit for improving the road system during the next election.

I've done a lot of work with a very good NGO called HelpAge that helps villages set up Old People's Associations (OPAs). In connection with the OPAs, HelpAge organizes 'health camps' in which local public commune health departments visit villages to monitor blood pressure and give advice on diet, exercise, etc. Of course HelpAge pays the public officials to conduct the health camps, which is a good thing, since public health workers, paid only $30-$50 per month, are often not to be found at their regular jobs. The government trumpets its support for the health camps and has recommended that they be expanded to all villages in Cambodia. However, the government spends nothing on the health camps while taking credit for them. The camps are not sustainable, because when HelpAge pulls the plug on funding, the health camps will cease to exist.

Interviewing old people for HelpAge International

People who work on the big projects with government tell me that a lot of the project money never manages to get spent. At the end of the project, the number one criterion for evaluating the project is how much of the money has been spent, regardless of the actual results of the project. Reminds me of an old joke that might be told about Cambodia: the Cambodian Finance Minister was visiting the Finance Minister of another nearby country.

Foreign FM: See that bridge over there?

Cambodian: Yes.

Foreign FM (points to his pocket): 20% of the money went in here.

The Cambodian was impressed. When the foreign FM paid a return trip to Cambodia,

Cambodian: See that bridge over there?

Foreign FM: No, I don't see anything

Cambodian (points to his pocket): 100%.

I should also mention the work that NGOs are working with government to stop trafficking and sex tourism. Much of this work is very good, but there are some horror stories where one or two well-known NGOs are targeting possibly innocent foreign males to have them thrown into jail. Why? Because the NGOs, especially the Cambodian Women's Crisis Centre (CWCC), can show off to its international donors the results of its work in putting away evil sex predators. Sounds good, but listen to some of the methods used by CWCC, as reported in Australia in the Brisbane Times

> An Australian national has been found dead in his Cambodian jail cell, officials and family said today.
>
> Bart "Lucky" Lauwaert, a former teacher, had been serving a 20-year sentence for child sex offences in a case which was spearheaded by local rights group, the Cambodian Women's Crisis Centre (CWCC).

In a phone interview from Siem Reap prison, 400km north of the capital, after his last avenue of appeal was closed last month, Lauwaert again alleged he had been "set up" by people trying to garner donor aid from high-profile arrests and threatened suicide.

The case became controversial in 2006 when all the girls who had originally testified against the men in Siem Reap court recanted in the Cambodian Appeals Court, claiming they were promised financial rewards by the CWCC for their testimony.

Then-Australian Justice Minister Chris Ellison also ordered a full investigation into any Australian aid supplied to the CWCC.

The CWCC strenuously denies any wrongdoing, pointing to continued funding from highly reputable donors including America's USAid and a decade-long record dotted with awards and accolades.

A former Siem Reap judge, Tan Senarong, has publicly admitted his sister works for the CWCC Siem Reap, but denies she works in any area of the organisation where a conflict of interest could arise.

One foreigner remains in jail from a CWCC-spearheaded investigation.

New Zealand national Graham Robert Cleghorn has also claimed he was set up by powerful interests wanting his valuable land in Siem Reap, which has been sold since his 2004 arrest.

He is also in poor health, according to his family and a doctor's report, and has also threatened suicide if his appeals fail.

The CWCC founder and director in charge when the foreign men were arrested, Oung Chanthol, resigned last year, citing fatigue over the controversy and a need to spend more time with her children.

I saw these methods first-hand when one of our foreign teachers in Battambang was accused by an NGO of raping a three-year-old in the school toilet. The guy was not even at school the day in question, and teachers testified that they were with the girl the whole morning. Everyone agrees that there is absolutely no evidence against the guy, who is happily married with four children, but the NGO persists with its persecution of him.

Are these isolated events? Not at all. Framing of foreigners is quite common. Here is another story of the framing of an expat whom the article (from the website Inquisition21) calls X.X.

X.X. had his title in the name of a shop owner and hotel supplier named ABC (name removed by editor).

ABC had been a school teacher. X.X. did not know that the father of the judge, Tan Senarong, had been the head teacher at the school or that Tan Senarong and his sister were both students at the same school where ABC had taught. (Tan Senarong was the judge that convicted both Cleghorn and X.X. and who was accused by Cleghorn of attempted blackmail before his own conviction. Tan Senarong's sister was head of the Cambodian Women's Crisis Centre (**CWCC**), which set up both men.)

At some stage ABC realized that if X.X. was extradited to his Home Country, or if he died in prison, then he (ABC) would be a very wealthy man, worth close to one million dollars.

… two boys arrived at the XXX Centre; the restaurant X.X. was operating on his property. The two boys asked if they could watch TV. He refused and ordered them to leave his room. One pulled off his underwear. The other one ran to the gate, unlocked it, and shouted "Help!" **Outside were three women from the CWCC (one who had come up from Phnom Penh), three foreign journalists with video cameras and eight policemen.** They burst into the room.

They removed his karma [*sic*], handcuffed him, and filmed him naked with the two boys who were now also naked. The staff member refused to co-operate with the set up. **He was offered $10,000 if he would sign a complaint and say he was sodomized by X.X..** He refused and was taken to the holding cells where he was stripped naked and humiliated, and when he still refused he was stunned with a stun baton on his genitals. He still refused. He was then charged with procuring boys for X.X. to rape. Most of the cases that followed this event follow the same pattern that is layed out by the NGO's.

At the police station the tables were filled with celebration beer and food, a small gift for the police having captured a paedophile. Both the **CWCC** and the journalists, who had helped arrange the set up and participated in it, attended this celebration.

Upon his arrest, his lawyer immediately requested a temporary release based on the fact that there was no evidence to support the accusations, but this request was turned down by the District Court of Siem Reap.

No expatriate male is safe from these set-ups. My advice to expat males is to stay well clear of children. This is not always easy, because when I visit orphanages or schools, children often rush up and try to hold my hand. I get away immediately, because there might be an NGO spy with a camera. A photograph of an expat holding the hand of a child could be used to frame the expat.

I have observed many idealistic foreigners who come to Cambodia, see the overwhelming and gut-wrenching needs, and set up their own projects or organizations. Gradually, they get sucked into the funding game, and spend more and more of their time raising funds. In the end, they become obsessed by funding and expanding their empire, and they may resort to more and more dubious methods. Power corrupts.

Similarly, foreign NGO workers come to Cambodia and find a comfortable, cushy lifestyle that they want to protect and perpetuate. They naturally would never recommend that their project has finished its mandate, or perhaps that the project is a failure. Many of these foreigners are being paid a Western salary of many thousands of dollars per month, easily twenty to thirty times the salaries their local counterparts. They have to justify themselves, usually by pointing out that they are highly trained development professionals that are in short supply on the job market, and that they must be paid high incentive pay to get them to come out to a 'hardship post' in what is painted as a hellhole in Cambodia.

At the end of my first project in Cambodia, I wrote up a glowing report demonstrating that we had achieved all our objectives. To my dismay, my boss told me that you must never make such claims because you want to prolong your project. The correct report states "The project achieved some of its objectives, but due to factors beyond our control, some objectives require more time." (In other words, a lucrative extension of the project)

The foreign experts also get special perks, in addition to their 20-30 multiples of local salaries, which must seem unfair to their local counterparts. At Handicap International, I noticed that the expats would drive the HI Land Cruisers around as if the cars were their own. The local staff members, however, were not allowed to drive the HI motorcycles home for lunch.

Despite the fact that NGOs spend a lot of money on themselves rather than on the actual poor people they are expected to serve, you can still argue that the current system does provide benefits for the poor people, albeit inefficiently. Even if only one project dollar in ten actually makes its way to the locals, that dollar is still doing some good, so why should anyone complain?

On the other hand, shouldn't we be worrying about dependency? Are local people and governments coming to depend on the aid they are receiving instead of learning to help themselves? Surely the donors are aware of this problem, so they are eager to embrace project titles such as "Self-help project," even if the project has nothing to do with self-help. The most dependent of all the recipients is the government. They don't have to provide services for the poor or salaries for their own workers if the NGOs are willing to do it for them. Shouldn't the government take some responsibility for education, health, and social services? I often hear the complaint that NGOs are allowing the government to abdicate its responsibilities.

The opposite argument is that the kleptocratic Cambodian government is not going to live up to its responsibilities under any circumstances. If NGOs stopped providing teachers or supplements to government teacher salaries, the government wouldn't do anything anyway. A lot of NGOs recognize this problem and provide assistance to 'governance' projects, but in the end, those projects just pay off government officials, and the money thrown at these projects ends up in officials' pockets without any improvement in 'governance.'

I have learned from personal experience that it is difficult to help people. I have had many friends who have been in personal trouble, but I am usually saddened when I am unable to help them. Likewise, NGOs find it difficult to induce people to break with tradition, inertia, and ingrown habits. For example, adult literacy programs around the world, and in Cambodia in particular, have often been unsuccessful, because adults who express a desire to learn to read usually find that it takes more effort than they expected, or that other activities in a busy life interfere with the continuous work over a period of time.

To solve this problem, a literacy program in which I participated decided to offer 'incentives' to its adult learners, by giving them sacks of rice. In other words, they paid the adults to attend class. I believe that such practices breed dependency. Any new launch of a literacy program will be met with a demand for rice. "If you don't give us rice, we won't come to your classes." The NGO will have to back down from this blackmail, because they need the participation of the 'beneficiaries' in order to justify their project funding, and consequently, their own high salaries.

So where do I come down on the issue of NGOs? Should we simply throw out all the NGOs? No, I guess not. They provide a service, even though only a small percentage of their budget is spent on the actual service. Without the NGOs, the government officials and their cronies would just rip off the needy people even more than at present and make them even more miserable than they are now. It's a protection racket. Government, in a sense, extorts a bribe from the NGOs for the right to provide partial protection for the people against the depredations of government officials. NGOs must, however, continually fight against the demands of the rich and powerful for a greater and greater share of the pie.

ECONOMICS

Construction Boom in Battambang

The Cambodian economy is booming. Construction projects are going up everywhere – 5-star hotels, shopping malls, and luxury apartment complexes are springing up like mushrooms. The following World Bank chart gives a snapshot of Cambodia's economy.

	2004	2005	2006	2007	2008	2009	2010	2011
GNI per capita, PPP(current international $)	1,250	1,440	1,630	1,830	1,960	1,970	2,080	2,230
Total Population (Millions)	13.19	13.36	13.52	13.67	13.82	13.98	14.14	14.31
GDP (Millions US$)	5,338	6,293	7,274	8,640	10351	10401	11242	12830
GDP Growth (annual %)	10.34	13.25	10.77	10.21	6.69	0.09	5.96	7.07
Life Expectancy at birth, total (years)	59.43	59.98	60.53	61.06	61.58	62.07	62.54	62.98

Notice that the GDP has doubled in eight years, and even the per capita income has nearly doubled. After dropping to nearly zero during the world recession, growth has returned to 7% per year.

Foreigners who return to Phnom Penh or Siem Reap after years of absence are astounded at how modern these places have become. There are now good highways connecting the major cities, while old-timers can remember the bad old days of simply horrendous roads. In fact, when I first arrived in 1995, it was impossible to travel by road from Phnom Penh to Siem Reap because the Khmer Rouge were still active in large areas north of the Tonle Sap.

Under this gloss of good news, however, there are some hidden dark spots. In a nutshell, the rich are getting richer and the poor are getting poorer. That increased inequality seems to be a feature of economic growth in developing countries. In fact, I could go so far as to claim that increased inequality is a *prerequisite* for growth. That is, you have to give the rich guys the freedom to get richer at the expense of the poor people. Maybe that's why communism failed: countries took from the rich and gave to the poor so that everyone was equal, which turned out to mean 'equally poor.'

In Cambodia the system of 'take from the poor and give to the rich' has reached outrageous proportions. This is especially evident in the 'land grabs' that are taking place all over the country. Here's how it works.

After the Khmer Rouge era the system of land ownership or titles had collapsed. Most rural dwellers had been displaced by the violence and had settled on farmland without clear title to the land. These squatters can easily be thrown off the land that they cannot prove that they own. High government officials can grant land to their cronies, who then bring in their bulldozers and demolish the existing houses on the land in favor of large-scale agricultural projects.

In the eastern tribal areas of Rattanakiri and Mondulkiri, the ethnic minorities living in the forests have no idea of land title; they have lived there for centuries on their traditional land. Along comes a rich businessman and shows them a document (likely in a language they cannot read) that tells them to vacate the land for a large rubber plantation. The bulldozers arrive, the forest is cleared, government troops assist in throwing out the residents from their ancestral homes. In 2012 troops went into a village in Kratie Province and murdered a 14-year old girl they found hiding in the basement of her home. The villagers who had tried to resist were arrested, and one leader named Mam Sonando was charged with forming a 'secessionist movement' to break away from Cambodia. His sentence of 20 years in prison was labeled by various human rights groups as "a prisoner of conscience ... absolutely outrageous" (Amnesty International), "politically motivated"(Cambodian Centre for Civil Rights), and "raises severe doubts about the impartiality and independence of the court"(European Union).

In fact, given the corruption of the legal system, it is easy for a rich crony to forge a title and to take land away from someone who actually owns the land. This is why I counsel foreigners not to start a business or otherwise invest in Cambodia. The higher-ups may allow you to eke out a survival existence, but if you actually start to make serious money, they can just step in and say, "I'll take that." Without a functioning legal system or the rule of law, you have no recourse. They can just take anything away from you.

Land grabbing is happening all over Cambodia, throwing thousands and thousands of poor people out of their homes. Where do they go? In some cases the government promises them relocation onto new land. More often than not, this new land is useless, for example in the middle of a malarial swamp or a place that floods during the rainy season. Also, these marginal lands are remote and too far for the residents to commute to jobs in towns or cities, or else there are no roads to these places to bring in commerce. Eventually, the relocated persons cannot survive and trickle off to parts unknown.

Those parts unknown are often cities like Poipet, on the border with Thailand. Thousands of displaced persons end up there to find menial jobs pushing overloaded carts across the border. They live in absolutely disgusting conditions along the stinking O Chrou creek, and are exploited and mistreated because they have no rights or no protectors, as required by the feudal hierarchy.

The agricultural lands that have been taken over by the crony capitalists can now produce cash crops like rubber, corn, cassava, or rice. These can be very profitable to the new owners, especially when commodity prices rise. For example, the global switch to bio-diesel creates a demand for cassava and other ethanol-producing plants. All these profits contribute to the rise in Cambodian GDP, and they are certainly more growth-enhancing than the former traditional subsistence survival.

This situation is an excellent example of how GDP growth is achieved by allowing the rich to get richer at the expense of the poor. Cambodian GDP can grow at 7% per year on the backs of these land grabs, and the international economists applaud Cambodia for its ability to get its economic act together.

These same international economists are even more pleased when they jet into Phnom Penh and see the new buildings, the construction, and other modern improvements that demonstrate how much progress is being made in Cambodia. Of course, they don't see the hovels in the mud of Poipet or the peasants relocated to a flood zone.

On the industrial front, Cambodia has for the past 20 years attracted garment manufacturers to take advantage of the low wages paid to the thousands of girls who flock to these factories for work. For some years, Cambodia could not compete with China, whose artificially low currency made Chinese exports cheap on world markets. Cambodia tried to compete by assuring multinationals that Cambodia would treat its workers correctly and transparently and would allow for open labor practices. There may have been some truth to this claim, but there were plenty of instances where workers complained of mistreatment.

Cambodia guarantees freedom of expression and the right of peaceable assembly. However, you must get government permission to stage a demonstration, and this permission is almost always denied. So any demonstrations are in effect illegal and are met with police brutality.

The labor movement suffered a severe setback in 2004, when labor activist Chea Vichea was assassinated. Sara Colm of Human Rights Watch noted

> This killing will not only send shockwaves through the labor movement, but it may also silence and intimidate opposition activists and journalists....This assassination will surely exacerbate the climate of fear for workers, journalists, environment and human rights activists who speak out or publicly demonstrate to express their views... Unfortunately, Cambodia has a poor track record in bringing to justice the perpetrators of political killings. The Cambodian authorities must take immediate steps to enforce the law and protect those who struggle for basic freedoms including labor rights.

Environmental activists who oppose the massive destruction of Cambodian forests are also targeted. In late 2012 Chut Vutty was shot and killed at point blank range by an official of the Timber Green logging company. The local judge ruled that the killing was 'accidental' and the killer walked free, to the howls of such human rights watchdogs as Reporters Without Borders ("A botched investigation has been quickly closed because the authorities did not want to draw attention to environmental problems for which powerful people are to blame,"), or Global Witness ("can only be described by as the latest effort to silence those who criticize the government's abuse of the country's land"), or Licadho ("a mockery of justice from day one").

The discouraging aspect of all this government heavy-handedness is that it is getting worse, not better. When I first came to Cambodia, the government used excuses like "Well, you can't expect a new government to be perfect in the field of human rights, especially after the Khmer Rouge era. Give us time to improve. We are working on the problems and hope to see a gradual improvement of human rights in Cambodia." Now, 20 years after the UNTAC elections, the human rights situation continues to deteriorate, as the ruling party becomes stronger and stronger, and hence less and less moved by criticism.

China is experiencing a rise in salaries of garment workers, and the Chinese yuan has gradually been allowed to appreciate against the US Dollar. That means that Cambodia is more competitive against China. The goal of making Cambodia fill the 'good guy' niche is not as important as it was a decade ago. Therefore, Cambodia doesn't have to be the good guy any more. Cambodia now ranks among the worst labor abusers, along with Bangladesh, in the 'race to the bottom.' In fact, after the Bangladesh tragedy, according to the New York Times (16/05/13) companies are pulling out of the politically incorrect Bangladesh and looking for new countries to exploit cheap labor. Of course, they are looking at Cambodia. However, just last week, according to the article, a shoe factory in Central Cambodia collapsed, killing three workers.

Recently there has been a spate of mass faintings in garment factories. The Asia Floor Wage network reported that "In 2011 year alone, the Free Trade Union has reported some 2,300 workers fainting in 5 Cambodian factories."

LTO Cambodia reports, "These factory workers are largely poor young women, often country girls, working in gray, stuffy, unpleasant conditions, homesick, pressured by family and harsh supervisors and doing mind-numbingly repetitive work for very little money (averaging $55-$61/month,) often for long hours."

Connect the neglect for worker safety with a construction scene in which legal oversight is weak and incompetent construction officials merely buy their contracts, and you have a recipe for a factory collapse like the one in Bangladesh in May, 2013. There are major accidents waiting to happen in Cambodia.

Another less dramatic danger for the economy is that aspiring entrepreneurs are borrowing huge amounts of money for their construction projects. International financial institutions like the IMF are warning that a credit bubble could form and then burst. From my viewpoint in Battambang, I see all the luxury hotels going up and I wonder who is going to stay in all those luxury rooms. What will happen if several hotels cannot attract customers and cannot repay those loans, and the banks go bust. The whole house of cards could collapse.

There is a theory among the ubiquitous conspiracy theorists that this construction is laundered ill-gotten money seeking to find an outlet. In this scenario, it doesn't matter much whether the hotels fill any of their rooms or not. In fact, some of the same conspiracy theorists claim that laundered money is also used to pay hotel bills, as clients could run up huge hotel bills and pay in laundered cash.

In summary, it appears that Cambodia's economy is growing precisely because of the exploitation of its resources, both natural and human, by a corrupt system of crony capitalism. One question that remains is the extent of the trickle-down effect. What benefits are trickling down from the rich elite to the exploited poor? Clearly, the infrastructure is improving. The system of highways has improved remarkably, and this system can be used by all Cambodians, rich or poor. There are also more school buildings for children to attend, even though the quality of their education is debatable. There is a growing middle class of shopowners, as well as clerks, receptionists, and secretaries who cater to the upper class. So there is some trickle down, but try telling that to the thousands of victims of the land grabs who are living miserable lives in hellholes like Poipet.

48

CHINA

Chinese graves and Khmer stupa

Cambodia's relationship with China is complex. If we go back to the 1970s, China was the main supporter of the Khmer Rouge and Pol Pot. During the years 1975-79, an estimated 2 million Khmers died, mostly by starvation. How could this happen if the people spent long hours cultivating rice? The obvious answer is that rice production was enormous, but all the rice went to China in return for weapons, while the people starved. When I worked in the last area in Cambodia controlled by the Khmer Rouge, I met many, many former KR cadres with pictures on their walls of their training trips to China.

A Wikipedia entry claims that most of the top brass under the Khmer Rouge were actually Sino-Khmer, including Pol Pot, Ieng Sary, Khieu Samphan, Nuon Chea, Tol Sleng prison director Duc, and Ta Mok.

Clearly, China has the blood of a couple million Khmers on its hands, and yet now, Cambodia's best international friend is China.

Many present-day Khmers whose families were decimated by the Chinese-backed KR now love the Chinese, and Cambodia is on its way to becoming a willing Chinese colony.

If you travel from Phnom Penh towards Sihanoukville, you will see mile after mile of Chinese factories, with all the signs in Chinese. You wonder what country you are in. There are many Chinese products in shops, and many Chinese channels on television.

In schools, more and more students are learning Chinese. This could be for two reasons: first, there are a lot of Khmer-Chinese who are ethnically at least part-Chinese, but who have never learned the language. Many want to connect with their Chinese cultural roots. Second, with the increasing Chinese economic influence, people are seeing the need to communicate with Chinese businessmen.

Chinese School, Battambang

Chinese and Khmer are Asian cultures, and while there are differences, they have much more in common than Khmer and Western cultures. Khmer Buddhist culture, in its pacifism, avoidance of confrontation, and hierarchical social system, has a lot in common with the Confucian ethic. The Confucian notions of filial piety and obedience to authority are very Cambodian. In addition, both China and Cambodia are coming off dark eras in their histories – the Cultural Revolution and the Khmer Rouge holocaust. These dark, violent reminders give both countries an abhorrence of plunging back into violence.

The government leaders, like Prime Minister Hun Sen, are warming to the Chinese influence, even though they were at the head of the Vietnamese-backed (and hence ferociously anti-Chinese) government of the 1980s, and now have done a 180 degree about face and are working hand-in-glove with the Chinese.

Cambodian leaders over the past 2000 years have jumped back and forth between perceived enemies, enlisting support from one side, then from the other, usually Thailand and Vietnam. Modern Cambodia is no different. Think of the mercurial Sihanouk, who supported even the Khmer Rouge in an attempt to retain a semblance of his personal power. Thus Hun Sen has had no difficulty being a member of the Chinese-backed Khmer Rouge, then jumping to the Vietnamese Heng Samrin regime (when in 1988 he stated "China was the root of everything that was evil in Cambodia,") and now back to the pro-Chinese stances he has increasingly been taking.

China is now the power in Asia, and Cambodia knows on which side its bread is being buttered. Chinese companies are pouring investment dollars into Cambodia at an astonishing rate. Chinese capital is behind the construction boom in factories, hotels and shopping malls. The Chinese government is financing roads, dams, and other infrastructure projects around Cambodia. When the Chinese-built road was built from Stung Treng to the Lao border, one expat remarked, "How convenient for Chinese tanks to roll into Phnom Penh!"

Cambodia and many other countries, especially in Africa, are happy to deal with China because of the no-strings-attached policies of China. These policies take two forms.

First, Western foreign aid has always been tied to improvements in human rights. America will give foreign aid or investment if Cambodia will promise to stop jailing opposition politicians. Can you imagine China complaining about the treatment of dissidents? Chinese aid, therefore, gives Cambodia cover for its growing human rights abuses, while Western leverage is forced to take a back seat.

Second, Western governments and companies have transparency and anti-corruption clauses written into contracts. Chinese contracts do not. China plays the corruption-cronyism game with Cambodia, so that the Cambodian elite and powerful are awarded the contracts with the usual into-the-pocket percentage never coming to light.

Many of today's government leaders are part-Chinese, according Wikpedia including the first lady Bun Rany, the Minister of Commerce Cham Prasith, and the Minister of Defence Tea Banh. An interesting article by Vohar Cheath for Radio Free Asia claims that "Hun Sen's family has Chinese roots." The Asia Times quotes Hun Sen as calling China "Cambodia's most trustworthy friend."

Cheath also discusses the numbers of Sino-Khmer in Cambodia. They were welcomed by Norodom Sihanouk, who established diplomatic relations with China in 1958 and was a close friend of Zhou-en Lai. From a high of 425,000 in the 1960s, the number fell dramatically during the KR regime, not because of racial discrimination, but because the Chinese community were the merchants and government officials whom the KR were trying to stamp out of their utopian rural society. The number of Chinese may have dropped to 61,000 by the end of the 1970s. When the Vietnamese took over, there was more active racial discrimination, since Vietnam was an enemy of China. From this era onward it is difficult to count the numbers of Sino-Khmer, mostly because under the Vietnamese they were forced to change their names to more Khmer sounding names. Today, therefore, many Cambodians with Khmer names may have Chinese ancestors. Cheath sites statistics to claim that there are 700,000 Sino Khmers in the country today.

After the UNTAC elections, the West tried to promote democracy and the rule of law, and so they backed the election winners, FUNCINPEC, under Prince Rannaridh . When he was overthrown by Hun Sen in 1997, the West described it as a coup d'etat and withdrew support for the government. Only the Chinese supported Hun Sen, and he has been faithful to them to this day.

If you estimate Cambodia's population at 14 million, 700,000 represents only about 5%. This is quite low, although the Chinese business and political clout is surly much more than 5% of the power or the GDP of the country.

One of the benefits that China receives in return for all its apparent aid is support in political forums. This was evident in 2012 when the ASEAN summit was held in Phnom Penh. Most of the members wanted to join together to present a united front to oppose China's various land claims around the South China Sea. China preferred to divide and conquer, that is, to deal with each country and each land claim separately, since China is vastly more powerful than any one small Southeast Asian state. China would be at a disadvantage if all those states banded together to oppose Chinese expansionism.

So in its influential position of Conference Chair, Cambodia, with no territorial disputes with China, forbade the meeting from bringing up the land claims in front of the general meeting, thereby serving as China's pawn. Cambodia also is instrumental in isolating Taiwan as part of Beijing's 'one-China policy."

Cheath's article bemoans the subtle and growing influences of Chinese culture on Cambodia. He claims that chopsticks are a recent addition to the Cambodian dining customs, and that for breakfast Chinese noodles have replaced more traditional Khmer dishes like those sticky-rice cakes called Num Ansohm.

What frightens me is that Cambodia could return to something like the Chinese Protectorate of the Khmer Rouge regime of the 1970s. Sounds far-fetched? Let me paint a picture of how it could happen.

Khmer society has always reminded me of the feudalism of medieval Europe. Remember those pyramidal diagrams from your old school which showed the king on top, the pyramid of barons and knights below, and the suffering serfs at the bottom? Through a system of patronage, each level was responsible to the higher level for providing either produce to the manor, or else soldiering in times of war. In return, the lower was given protection by the higher level. Cambodia's system of patronage reminds me of that, in that higher-ups seem to 'own' their vassals. I've always been amazed at how company employees are required by their bosses to perform personal services such as wait on table at the boss's daughter's wedding. No one ever claims, "That's not in my contract."

Not many people, even Cambodians, have ever heard of Kos Kralor District in Battambang Province. Located south of Moung Russey, this was one of the last holdouts of the Khmer Rouge. When the KR capitulated, the government offered free land to homesteaders to go develop Kos Kralor. The trouble was, there is almost no water there, and a lot of hopeful farmers were not able to grow anything. However, the district was never fully controlled by the government, but rather was under a sort of warlord system of generals and powerful families, who could build canals or ponds and thereby control the water supply. Gradually, the poor farmers sold out to the warlords and became medieval serfs to work the land in return for protection. That is the situation in Kos Kralor today, which may serve as a model for the future of Cambodia.

All over Cambodia, the powerful cronies of the regime are grabbing land from the poor farmers. They are producing rice and other agricultural products for export to – where else? – China. In return,

China sends luxury goods to the controlling elite. The poor are getting poorer. They have the choice of working practically as slaves for the landowners, or else migrating to hellholes like Poipet, where they are equivalent to slaves anyway.

Could Cambodia descend into a situation whereby the power-brokers merely control the shipment of agricultural produce to China, while China sends luxury goods to the rich and powerful, and the starving serfs toil in conditions reminiscent of the 1970s? If you don't believe this, you should go to Poipet and see the horrible living conditions of the people (might as well call them slaves) who push the products across the border all day. Or go to some of the places where people who have been forced off their land by powerful land grabbers and are now forced to live in malarial swamps or deserts where nothing grows. Is that the future of Cambodia as a Chinese colony?

CAMBODIA'S FUTURE

Chinese-built dam

"The trend is your friend." That's a phrase used by investors in buying stocks, but it can also apply to predicting Cambodia's future. I have been following Cambodia since 1995, and the trends since then have been fairly clear for all to see. It makes sense to extrapolate those trends over the next ten to twenty years.

First, the rich-poor divide has increased greatly, not only in Cambodia but worldwide. With the collapse and discrediting of communism, world economists have concluded that the path to economic growth is through giving the rich free rein to pursue their wealth at the expense of the poor. This method has been successful in Cambodia, whose economy is growing at over 7% per year, even though that 7% is going to the richest, while the poor are being thrown off their traditional lands so the crony capitalists can produce cash crops.

This trend is likely to continue. This means that we will see more cash crops produced by large agricultural conglomerates run by Chinese capitalists in league with local politicians. The GDP will continue to grow.

Likewise, Cambodia's industry, notably the garment industry, will continue to grow to the profit of the crony capitalists. This will be especially true when working conditions and salaries will improve in China, so that Cambodia can occupy its place at the bottom of the chain. Chinese capital will move into Cambodian industry, creating an increasingly opaque, corrupt, and dangerous situation in the factories. With lack of oversight, and lack of Western watchdogging, conditions can only worsen. However, as farmers are thrown off their land, there will still be thousands of girls from struggling families streaming in from the provinces in search of work under any conditions.

Politically, the trend over the past 20 years has been towards consolidation of power in the hands of the Cambodian People's Party. Opposition politicians have either discredited themselves or have been persecuted, jailed, exiled, or assassinated in an increasing climate of impunity.

This concentration of power is likely to continue, as it has been successful for the vested interests and the opposition has been largely eliminated. The Monarchy can be allowed to continue as window dressing without any real clout. While the current King Sihamoni is regarded as compliant to the regime, The Prime Minister is looking more like a king. He has awarded himself with a whole string of honorary epithets: one must not just refer to him as "Prime Minister", but as "His Excellency Prime Minister Samdech Akka Moha Sena Padei Decho Hun Sen." A decade ago, only the photograph of King Sihanouk and his wife Monique Monineath were displayed in public offices, but then Hun Sen's photograph crept in, and now it is placed on equal footing with the king, and his wife Bun Rany also appears as a clear reference and parallel to Sihanouk's favorite wife.

In the months during and after Sihanouk's funeral, Hun Sen made new references to his claim to royalty. He claimed to have a dream in which Angkor-era kings spoke to him. He also claimed there was a former king named Hun. Finally, at the cremation of Sihanouk, various people were having problems lighting the funeral pyre; in the end, only Hun Sen magically was able to light the sacred fire.

So we will see the current leaders assuming more royal and autocratic roles. Even the deputy prime ministers and other power brokers are being groomed for royal roles. There is considerable inter-family marriage, such as between Hun Sen's progeny and that of Sar Kheng, reminding one of the medieval intermarrying of royal families. Most of the sons and daughters of Hun Sen and other high officials are now entered onto lists of candidates for the upcoming elections, ensuring a dynasty of support over the next several decades.

On the other hand, the rulers need to present a façade of democracy, in order to continue receiving the development aid and the international affirmation that are so important to the regime. According to the OECD, Cambodia ranks 24th in the world in foreign aid as a percentage of GDP, just below Djibouti, at 12.5%. As described earlier, despite continued broken promises of reform by the government, foreign donors increase their aid every year, which has now surpassed a billion dollars, amounting to about half of the government budget.

In order to keep the foreign aid flowing, the government must allow the opposition parties to exist, however toothless they may be. There is talk that the CPP even gives financial support to the splinter parties, who make posters and banners for their campaign, but who either win no parliamentary seats at all, or else seats that support the CPP. There is a sort of unwritten code of what the opposition is allowed to criticize, with the understanding that if they cross the line, they can be charged with 'defamation' , i.e. criticism, which in the increasingly monarchical atmosphere, amounts to *lèse majesté*.

It is laughable to see the Sam Rainsy party (now transformed to the Khmer National Rescue Party) allowed to campaign for the 2013 elections, even as its founder and leader, Sam Rainsy, is in exile because the CPP would put him in jail if he returned.

We see, therefore, a future of a dictatorship disguised as a democratic monarchy. The Cambodian people will not change this trend because they are so fed up with the violence of the Khmer Rouge wars that they will allow themselves to be oppressed without risking violence.

This is the argument of Joel Brinkley's book, *Cambodia's Curse*. Brinkley's descriptions of the corruption and cronyism are in broad agreement with mine. The book has really pushed the buttons of some of my colleagues, who react emotionally against the book as total rubbish. I had to explore why they get so upset about Brinkley's book.

I think the main reason that people get emotional over this book is its apparent focus on 'blaming the victim', a phrase that is almost universally condemnable as a matter of principle. Cambodia was clearly a victim, for example, of United States bombing during the Vietnam War. This bombing is claimed to have driven Cambodia into the arms of the Khmer Rouge, leading to the horrors of the Pol Pot regime. Brinkley is criticized for minimizing the influence of the American bombing.

On the other hand, Sihanouk sided with the Khmer Rouge in order to regain his personal power, as evidenced by the famous photograph of Sihanouk with Pol Pot in Beijing. Should not Sihanouk bear some of the blame for the Khmer Rouge atrocities?

I believe that Brinkley gets it right in his conclusion that Khmer culture is different from other places around the world in that its gentle Buddhists allow bad things to happen to them without rebelling. There was no rebellion against the KR, according to Brinkley, because the Khmer people are just *too nice,* or rather, *too passive.* I have observed this phenomenon in other countries. I lived in Mozambique, which the Portuguese explorers called the "*Terra de boa gente*", or "land of nice people." It's true: the Mozambicans are a lot like the Khmer, with their charming smile and easy-going nature. But they let the Western-backed RENAMO commit horrible atrocities without much of a fight-back. Closer to Cambodia, the Burmese people are very charming and pleasant, also pacifist Buddhists, and look what happened to them.

It's pretty clear, therefore, that the charming Khmer people will allow the ruling kleptocrats to push them farther and farther; in fact, they will probably tolerate more abuse without rebellion than most people in the world. I can't help mentioning one of the best book titles about Southeast Asia: *Lands of Charm and Cruelty*, written by Stan Sesser back in 1994. That title describes Cambodia in a nutshell. Most visitors, however, see only the charm but miss the hidden cruelty.

As Cambodia falls more and more under Chinese hegemony, transparency and the rule of law will probably weaken considerably. This may cause Western companies to withdraw, as the cost of doing legitimate business increases. I don't see a MacDonalds in Phnom Penh any time soon. Western Governments and NGOs, on the other hand, will continue to pour development aid into the country, in order to maintain their own influence and leverage, but Cambodia will have to play the game by pretending to tolerate opposition parties in their pre-determined elections.

What could finally topple this system? I'd like to compare Cambodia to such strong-man rule as in Egypt, Libya, Iraq, and Iran (under the Shah). Almost every African country has needed a strongman to rule over ancient tribal hatreds. In all these countries, the strongman was able to bang together the heads of ethnic or religious groups to keep them from killing each other, for example, the way Saddam Hussein was able to keep the Sunnis and the Shias from each other's throats for a long time.

People in the above-mentioned countries have accepted the oppression of the dictator out of fear for the alternative: ethnic or sectarian massacres. Given the Cambodians' fear of the Pol Pot massacres, there is little doubt that they will allow the current regime to push them to the wall.

The current regime will probably come to an end something like the 'Arab Spring', but like the Arab Spring, it may take a very long time, like 20-30 years. The story of how the Arab Spring came about is still being discussed, but one important element was the unemployed and unskilled youth who felt that they had been disenfranchised. This could happen in Cambodia, given its virtually non-existent educational system. Expertise must be brought in from Vietnam and Thailand, and unemployed (and unemployable) Cambodian youth will begin to resent these well-trained foreigners doing the jobs that Cambodians have not been trained to do.

At the same time, when all the valuable land has been grabbed by the crony capitalists, the poor will be crowded onto marginal, non-productive land. There will be no place else to go. A movement like the Khmer Rouge may grow up to exploit the resentment of the rural poor against the corrupt urban rich. Of course, the poor have no power of their own. But some outside power like Vietnam or Thailand could exploit that resentment as a pretext for an invasion.

I can foresee a return to the centuries of Cambodian history, where weak despots turned to either Vietnam or Thailand to shore up their unpopular regimes. Much of Cambodia may return to Thailand or Vietnam. After all, the entire north and west of Cambodia belonged to Thailand right into the 20th century. We might eventually see a division of Cambodia along the Mekong River, where the east would either belong to, or be a protectorate of Vietnam, while the west would 'belong' to Thailand. But even if this division takes place, the world will demand a nominal existence for Cambodia, the way Cambodia has been allowed to exist for centuries.

One should not neglect the possibility of some other game-changing 'black swan event.' For example, suppose Hun Sen were somehow incapacitated. Would there be a full scale civil war between factions of the CPP? Would a new leader take the country in a different direction? Probably not, because the old-boy network would still control the economy. The military is in cahoots with the business community; in fact, many of the elite are the generals.

Cambodia is a surreal country. Foreigners who either visit or live in Cambodia are constantly asking themselves, "Can this really exist?" To see what from outward appearances is an educational system, but in reality is make-believe, or to see what from outward appearances is a judicial system, but in reality is make-believe, is to find oneself in a sort of Twilight Zone. This fantasy world is likely to continue and to become even more surreal.

Related books by Ray Zepp

The Cambodia Less Traveled (1996)

A Field Guide to Cambodian Pagodas (1997)

A Field Guide to Siem Reap Pagodas (1998)

Around Battambang (2006)

Studies in Cambodian Leadership (2007)

Jataka Stories for English Language Students (2009)

Cambodian History for Students of English (2012)

The author can be contacted at zepp@rocketmail.com